WELCOME TO NURSING

A 30 day prayer and devotional guide for new nurses.
Volume 1

TOMEKIA Y. LUCKETT, PHD, RN

Welcome to Nursing! A 30 day prayer and devotional guide for new nurses

Volume 1

By Tomekia Y. Luckett, PhD, RN

© 2018, Dr. Tomekia Yvette Enterprises LLC

www.drtomekia.com

Email: dr.tomekia@positionedforpurpose.com

Published by Dr.Tomekia Yvette Enterprises LLC

Cover Design by prodesignx

Author photograph by Beth Hemeter

(The Image Maker)

www.imagemakerinc.morephotos.net

I dedicate this book to the one who empowered and equipped me to write this devotional! You will forever be number one in my life. Thank you Lord, for, without you, I am nothing! Truly, with God, all things are possible (Matthew 19:26). Thank you for choosing me for this great purpose. I love you!

To all of my nurse colleagues around the world, this one is for you, you survived the greatest part of your journey, now it's time to begin your calling.

To my children, my sons, Tamerrious, Tamerrion, and Tamerrick, you three are my greatest joy and inspiration.

Contents

Introduction   vii

Day 1   1
Day 2   5
Day 3   9
Day 4   13
Day 5   17
Day 6   21
Day 7   25
Day 8   29
Day 9   33
Day 10   37
Day 11   41
Day 12   45
Day 13   49
Day 14   53
Day 15   57
Day 16   61
Day 17   65
Day 18   69
Day 19   73
Day 20   77
Day 21   81
Day 22   85
Day 23   89
Day 24   93
Day 25   97
Day 26   101
Day 27   105
Day 28   109
Day 29   113

Day 30   117

Prayers   121

Introduction

Welcome to the wonderful world of nursing! You are embarking on an exciting and rewarding career. As a veteran nurse and nurse educator, I am well acquainted with the challenges faced by newly licensed nurses. My hope is to equip you with the spiritual tools that you may need to continue in your calling as a nurse. God wants you to enjoy your new career, and walk in your calling. Never take lightly this wonderful calling that places you in a position to care for others. It is important to balance your work life with your personal life to prevent early burnout. One way to achieve balance is to spend time daily with God through prayer, studying the word, and listening to His voice for direction. The Lord wants to be a part of every aspect of your life, including your career.

This powerful devotional guide is designed with you, the busy, new nurse in mind. It is designed to remind you of the importance of spending time daily with God. I encourage you to take time before your shift and on days off to spend time with Him, and allow Him to prepare you for whatever your day might bring.

Day 1

~ A CALL TO SERVE ~

Day 1

A CALL TO SERVE

"The greatest among you will be your servant."
Matthew 23:11

The call to serve others is perhaps the greatest call from our Lord. As nurses, our very career is hinged upon us providing a service to our patients, families, and communities we are entrusted to care for. Today is a great and wonderful day! As you prepare for duty today, never forget your ultimate call to serve. Serving begins long before you enter into the building for your shift. Serving begins with an attitude, and a resolve to elevate others more highly than yourself. Serving can take many forms. Whether that is offering a cup of water, assisting with hygiene, or simply being a listening ear. Your kind deeds and encouraging words may make the world of difference to someone's life. Take the opportunity to serve someone and to reflect on the ray of sunshine you may bring to their life.

Prayer: Father, in the name of Jesus, I thank You for my call to serve. My desire is to glorify You through serving. I cannot do this alone, and

I need You, Holy Spirit to equip me to serve. Help me to serve with the humility of Jesus, and be his hands in the earth. In the mighty name of Jesus, Amen.

Day 2

~ WHEN MUCH IS GIVEN ~

Day 2

<hr>

WHEN MUCH IS GIVEN

*"But the one who does not know and does things deserving punishment
will be beaten with few blows. From everyone who has been given
much, much will be demanded; and from the one who has been
entrusted with much, much more will be asked."*
Luke 12:48

When much is given, much is also required! Remember while in
nursing school praying, and thinking of the day when you would
complete nursing school and become a nurse? The day is here. Do not
allow yourself to become overwhelmed with the hustle and bustle of
your career and forget how you succeeded and met your goal. How can
you help a fellow nurse? How can you display love and compassion in
your daily duties? How can you give back and demonstrate the love of
God in your day? Much is required of you, go the extra mile in your
calling as a nurse.

Prayer: Father, in the name of Jesus, I thank You for all of Your many
blessings. Help me to be ever thankful each and every day. In my work

and all that I do, help me to go the extra mile. In the name of Jesus, Amen.

Day 3

~ SURVIVING THE STORM ~

Day 3

SURVIVING THE STORM

*"God is our refuge and strength, an ever-present help in trouble.
Therefore we will not fear, though the earth give way and the
mountains fall into the heart of the sea,"*
Psalm 46: 1-2

Have you ever found yourself driving your car during a storm? How about riding down the road, and out of nowhere, a storm comes. When the rain becomes so heavy that you can hardly see the road, what should you do? If you pull over and stop, you will still be in the same spot standing still. However, if you make a decision to keep going, even if you have to go slowly, the storm will eventually run out of rain. In times when you are faced with a storm, or an unexpected challenge, just keep going! Don't give up in the storm, keep on going! Storms don't last forever!

Prayer: Father, in the name of Jesus help me to survive when I am in the midst of a storm. Give me strength to keep on going in the storm. Help me to endure, and endow me with the presence of Your precious Holy Spirit. In the mighty name of Jesus, Amen.

Day 4

~ RIGHT ON TIME ~

Day 4

RIGHT ON TIME

"For I know the plans I have for you," declares the Lord, "plans to prosper you and not to harm you, plans to give you hope and a future"
Jeremiah 29:11

Have you ever watched the lineup for airplanes departing on the runway? Different airlines, different planes, all headed for different destinations. The airplanes at the end of the line leave after the ones in the front of the line, BUT guess what? Each airplane will make it to its destination right on time. As a new nurse, do not become overwhelmed if others are progressing, and seem more knowledgeable than you, you will acquire the necessary skills and knowledge right on time. On average, many nurses express that it takes years before they become confident in their skills and feel as though they may understand their new role. Do not allow the timing of others to frustrate you, your competency level will grow, and you will get there right on time!

Prayer: Father, in the name of Jesus, help me to trust Your timing. I know that You have a good plan for my life and career. Help me to be more patient and surrender my plans to You, in the mighty name of Jesus, Amen.

Day 5

~ TRANSFORM YOUR MIND ~

Day 5

TRANSFORM YOUR MIND

"Do not conform to the pattern of this world, but be transformed by the renewing of your mind. Then you will be able to test and approve what God's will is—his good, pleasing and perfect will."
Romans 12:2

Have you ever been faced with negative self–talk, self-doubts, and fear? Have you ever watched an elephant being trained? When an elephant is being trained, during the time when it is a baby, a chain is tied to the leg to restrict its movement. When it attempts to move, it causes great pain to the elephant. And when it gets older, it won't even attempt to move because of the memory of the chain. So, a tiny rope can keep a large elephant bound, because it is bound in its mind.....Sometimes, the very thing that holds us back is actually in our mind! Think back, when did the mind shift happen for you? The shift from thinking like a student to a nurse. As a nurse, you now understand concepts like life before limb, and the necessity of airway, breathing and circulation. Take this same energy and apply it in any area of your mind that is holding you back. I challenge you today to transform and renew your mind!

Prayer: Father, in the name of Jesus, I surrender my mind, including my thoughts over to You. Help me to think on positive things and transform my mind daily with Your word. In the name of Jesus, Amen.

Day 6

~ BEFORE YOU CALL ~

Day 6

BEFORE YOU CALL

"Before they call I will answer; while they are still speaking I
will hear"
Isaiah 65:24

Have you ever been driving and had a group of first responders to race by? They have lights, sirens and the liberty to drive as fast as needed to make it to the scene. How quickly then can God dispatch an angel to your rescue? As a matter of fact, before you call, He will answer. An angel might be on the scene faster than you can blink an eye. Angels have been dispatched to your rescue, just hold on and keep the faith! Whatever fears and doubts that attempt to move your focus, remember that He will answer before you call.

Prayer: Father, in the name of Jesus, I thank You for always being present with me. I thank You for being the best part of my life. I thank You for answering, even before I call and I trust Your voice concerning my life. In the mighty name of Jesus, Amen.

Day 7

~ HOW MUCH FAITH ~

Day 7

God is not human, that he should lie,   not a human being, that he should change his mind. Does he speak and then not act?   Does he promise and not fulfill?
Numbers 23:19

How much faith? Have you ever faced an insurmountable obstacle? An obstacle which seemed literally larger than life? I am sure that you will have faced a number of obstacles during your time as a nursing student, but guess what? You made it, you completed the goal. How much faith would it take to simply walk around a giant wall seven times? The task was not to strike it, pray or anything. The task was simply to walk seven times. Think on how much faith Joshua and the children of Israel needed to march around the wall seven times! Most people would have questioned if it would eventually happen, and likely have given up after the first three or four times. Imagine marching 6 times and nothing was happening…Then, miraculously, the 7th time! The wall came down!

God is not a man that He should lie.... God cannot lie, if He said it, it will HAPPEN!!!!

How much faith do you have? Do you have faith enough to trust God when it looks like nothing will happen? Read Numbers 23:19 every time you're tempted not to believe His promises!

Prayer: Father, in the name of Jesus, thank You today for increasing my faith. Your word tells me that faith is confidence in what we hope for and assurance about what we do not see. Help me to trust You in every area of my life. In the mighty name of Jesus, Amen.

Day 8

~YOU HAVE THE POWER ~

Day 8

YOU HAVE THE POWER

"The tongue has the power of life and death, and those who love it will eat its fruit."
Proverbs 18:21

Death and life are in the POWER of the tongue: and they that love it SHALL eat the fruit thereof. You have the power in your mouth. Declare your day, declare your work week! Take a moment, and use your imagination. Imagine if each time you uttered a word, the words began to take on life and became active. The words had the power to literally do everything you empowered them to do with your mouth. Would you then be more careful of the words you so carelessly speak? Don't speak it UNLESS you want to see it happen! Never forget, you are blessed to have a mighty POWER source living on the inside, the Holy Spirit, He is God. May the power of God through the Holy Spirit who's mighty like a lion, yet humble as a lamb keep you! You have the power!

Prayer: Father, in the name of Jesus, help me to be ever mindful of the words I speak. I will speak life into my situation and trust You for all of my needs. In the mighty name of Jesus, Amen.

Day 9

~ HE IS THE AUTHOR ~

Day 9

HE IS THE AUTHOR

"For I know the plans I have for you," declares the Lord, plans to prosper you and not to harm you, plans to give you hope and a future."
Jeremiah 29:11

Nursing school tends to limit your time and ability to read for leisure. Take a second to think back on the last time you read a really, really good book. I mean a book so good, that you couldn't wait to read the ending. In those instances, you may cheat and read ahead, by starting from the ending and backtracking to the beginning. (A good author/writer often begins with the ending in mind). In life, we may have some good chapters, but then there are also the painful chapters. Never forget that God knows every single bit of your story, He holds the pen, and is writing your beautiful story. The author always knows what happened, what's presently happening and what's going to happen! Not one thing catches Him by surprise.... God already knows the ending and He is writing your story.

Prayer: Father, in the name of Jesus, thank You for being the author of my story. Help me to trust You with my life. Forgive me for the times when I doubted Your plan. In the mighty name of Jesus, Amen.

Day 10

~ GOD IS GREATER ~

Day 10

GOD IS GREATER

God is not human, that he should lie, not a human being, that he should change his mind. Does he speak and then not act? Does he promise and not fulfill?
Numbers 23:19

Have you ever taken the time to study the blessings and promises of Abraham? God told Abraham and Sarah of the promised seed at different times, but their response was the same. They were so great in disbelief, until it manifested and then they rejoiced. This is the kind of blessing that would be impossible UNLESS God orchestrated it. However, God is not moved by mountains nor impossibilities. He is the God that makes ALL things possible. He will call you rich, when you feel poor. He will call you blessed, when you feel cursed. He will speak life, when death is all around...... God isn't intimidated by mountains, He just moves them! As the story goes, the promise did come for Abraham and Sarah, though they were well advanced in age. God is getting ready to make you laugh! He's a great God!

Prayer: Father, in the name of Jesus, You are greater. You are greater than my every problem. Help me to glorify You in every way, and to believe all of your promises concerning me. I thank You for all of my many blessings. In the mighty name of Jesus, Amen.

Day 11

~ LET HIM FIX IT ~

Day 11

LET HIM FIX IT

"In his defense Jesus said to them, "My Father is always at his work to this very day, and I too am working."
John 5:17

Have you ever noticed a dead branch on a tree? The leaves do not look like the rest, they are withered, brown, and lifeless. One option would be to cut the dead branch off, to be sure those remaining on the tree would be green and vibrant. However, if you just take time and wait, what is dead will often fall off on its own. The problem will take care of itself. God doesn't need our help, He can't work while we are working too! Take your hands off, and let Him fix it....

Prayer: Father, in the name of Jesus, You know everything that concerns me. Help me to trust in Your plans and await Your promises. Lord, I will give my situation to You and place my life in Your hands. In the mighty name of Jesus, Amen.

Day 12

~ PATIENCE IS KEY ~

Day 12

PATIENCE IS KEY

"Let us not become weary in doing good, for at the proper time we will reap a harvest if we do not give up"
Galatians 6:9

Hurry, hurry, rush, and rush! We are living in a time when everything and everyone is fast paced. As you juggle your career and home life to meet all the daily demands, each day can be challenging. Have you ever been tempted while preparing a meal to turn the stove up high to make it cook faster? Often times, this makes a mess, as portions of the meal are undercooked while other portions are overcooked. Patience is key, quicker isn't necessarily better. Some blessings, like a really good meal take time! Be patient with God.

Prayer: Father, in the name of Jesus, teach me to patiently await Your promises. I trust Your plan for my life, and Your perfect timing. Give me strength to wait, and increase my patience in every area of my life. In the mighty name of Jesus, Amen.

Day 13

~TRUST HIS PLAN~

Day 13

TRUST HIS PLAN

"Trust in the Lord with all your heart and lean not on your own understanding; in all your ways submit to him, and he will make your paths straight.[a]
7 Do not be wise in your own eyes; fear the Lord and shun evil."
Proverbs 3:5-7

Have you ever tried to give medication to a pediatric patient or an uncooperative geriatric patient? I have tried a number of times and experienced great resistance. They would fight, claw, cry and scream like I was trying to kill them. When in actuality I was trying to help. Why is it then that we sometimes fight God's plan for our lives? We fight, kick, scream, and He's trying to help us all the time! He always has a plan in mind, and our best interest at heart. Make a special effort today to trust Him as never before, He never fails.

Prayer: Father, in the name of Jesus, I trust you. You have proven to me on countless occasions the power of your promises concerning me. I will continually trust you, and glorify your name. In the mighty name of Jesus, Amen.

Day 14

~FAITH IN THE UNSEEN~

Day 14

FAITH IN THE UNSEEN

*"Now faith is confidence in what we hope for and assurance about
what we do not see"*
Hebrews 11:1

Sometimes the weather man will report heavy fog, making it difficult to see the road in places. Just because the road isn't visible that doesn't mean it ceases to exist, the road is still there! Just like exercising your faith, just because you don't see it yet, it doesn't mean that you will never see it! God specializes in making the impossible, possible! You must SEE it BEFORE you SEE it! Don't let what you see, keep you blinded from what you do not see! Have faith today in the unseen.

Prayer: Father, in the name of Jesus, I believe You for that which remains unseen. I need You to increase my faith, and help me to believe Your words concerning my life. I have faith in You, and the power of the blood of Jesus. In the mighty name of Jesus, Amen.

Day 15

~PASS THE TEST ~

Day 15

PASS THE TEST

"Blessed is the one who perseveres under trial because, having stood the test, that person will receive the crown of life that the Lord has promised to those who love him"
James 1:12

Reflect back briefly on your time in nursing school, when there was the inevitable pop quiz. Sometimes the quiz was predictable, while other times, they were totally unexpected. The key to being successful on the quiz was to complete your readings and be prepared for class, just in case. Imagine failing to read or prepare for the quiz, and then boom, out of nowhere a pop quiz. What is the likelihood of passing? Very unlikely, Why? Because of a lack of preparation. A very valuable lesson learned is to always be ready because the test may come when you least expect it! It is important to pray without ceasing. Tests and trials will inevitably come, but prayer will help you be prepared. Withstand the test, because after the test there is victory!

Prayer: Father, in the name of Jesus, I declare victory over my tests. I believe that my test is already passed in the heavenly realm. Manifest the promise here on earth. In the mighty name of Jesus, Amen.

Day 16

~DOORS GOD OPENS ~

Day 16

DOORS GOD OPENS

"I know your deeds. See, I have placed before you an open door that no one can shut. I know that you have little strength, yet you have kept my word and have not denied my name."
Revelation 3:8

Congratulations, you have completed a major milestone by completing nursing school and beginning your career. A guiding question throughout your journey is, what's next? Which way should I go? Which setting best suits my career goals? Which doors should I open, and which ones should remain closed? Not all open doors are the right doors for us. Furthermore, not all good doors are God doors! Spending time in the presence of God will enhance your discernment. Listen to His voice; He cannot lie! He will lead you into truth, and the revelation of doors to open, and doors to close. Always remember, when He opens the door, no one can shut it!

Prayer: Father, in the name of Jesus, thank You for every door You have already opened in my life. I will await new doors and blessings in my life. Help me to know Your voice, and how to discern which doors come from You. In the mighty name of Jesus, Amen.

Day 17

~ GOD FIGHTS BATTLES ~

Day 17

GOD FIGHTS BATTLES

"The Lord will fight for you; you need only to be still"
Exodus 14:14

It is inevitable that at some point in life we will all be faced with a battle. The battle can be a battle of the mind, in the spirit realm, or it may manifest as a disagreement with an individual. Two people can't both win the same fight. It is a natural reaction when faced with a battle to fight back. The fight back can be through words or deeds. However, in a battle, there can only be one winner. We can choose to fight our battle or allow the Lord to fight for us. If you're fighting it, then God can't fight. So today's challenge is to trust God with all your battles.

Prayer: Father, in the name of Jesus, help me to trust You with all of my battles. I am victorious through Christ. Help me when faced with a battle to turn it over to You. Lord, I trust You. In the mighty name of Jesus, Amen.

Day 18

~ SPEAK TO THE MOUNTAIN ~

Day 18

SPEAK TO THE MOUNTAIN

"Truly I tell you, if anyone says to this mountain, 'Go, throw yourself into the sea,' and does not doubt in their heart but believes that what they say will happen, it will be done for them."
Mark 11:23

The height and depth of mountains make the climb seem impossible. In sincere ignorance, we may ask the Lord to help us climb the mountain. Climbing the mountain was never the intention of God, His intention was for us to simply speak to the mountain. You can speak to the biggest of mountains by faith, and watch it be removed by God.

Prayer: Father, in the name of Jesus, You are the mountain mover. Today, I surrender every mountain to You. I trust Your plans for me, and stand on Your word. In the mighty name of Jesus, Amen.

Day 19

~ SOAR HIGH ~

Day 19

SOAR HIGH

"Walk with the wise and become wise, for a companion of fools suffers harm"

Proverbs 13:20

An eagle in flight can recognize prey and see distances that are far away. Chickens however, must be within several inches to even recognize potential prey. Why is this important? The chicken cannot see what the eagle sees. Stop trying to get the person with a chicken mentality to try and understand the perspective of the eagle. The eagle who consistently hangs with chickens will soon forget how to fly. Watch your circle! You are a nurse, your calling is to touch lives. Your calling is extraordinary, and you are designed to soar, Soar High!

Prayer: Father, in the name of Jesus, help me to be selective in the company I keep. My heart longs to soar like an eagle in life and career. Lord, equip me with the knowledge of how to fulfill Your plan for my life. In the mighty name of Jesus, Amen.

Day 20

~ A NEW THING ~

Day 20

A NEW THING

Forget the former things; do not dwell on the past. 19 See, I am doing a new thing! Now it springs up; do you not perceive it? I am making a way in the wilderness and streams in the wasteland.
Isaiah 43:18-19

Have you ever really needed to clean out your closet? Some items are easy to part with especially if they are not your favorites. Some items though within yourself you rationalize keeping, especially if they have sentimental value. The more you try to hold on to what no longer fits, the more it prevents you from getting new things that truly fit. Just like the clothes, sometimes when you are trying to do new and better things, you must release some stuff. The more you release, the more room you make for God to bless you with. Release the old, in order to allow God to do a new thing.

Prayer: Father, in the name of Jesus, help me to let go of anything that could hinder Your plan for my life. Increase my wisdom and understanding of when to let go, and when to hold on. In the mighty name of Jesus, Amen.

Day 21

~ LET IT GO ~

Day 21

LET IT GO

"Every good and perfect gift is from above, coming down from the Father of the heavenly lights, who does not change like shifting shadows."

James 1:17

One of the most difficult tasks as a new or seasoned nurse is finding shoes that will be comfortable for work. Long, and tiring shifts make the need for proper fitting shoes a necessity. How about finding the perfect pair of shoes, and then discovering that they do not fit? Sometimes in life, like that shoe, things will come packaged as everything we want. The issue comes when you have to try and force something to fit that simply does not fit. It is more painful to try and force it to fit than to actually let go. No matter how bad you want it, if you have to force it to fit, and it causes you pain, take it off and let it go! Try out something new, maybe another pair of shoes or a new environment. Maybe it won't be as flashy or desirable as what you initially wanted, but it just might be your perfect fit! Every good and perfect gift is from above!

Prayer: Father, in the name of Jesus, thank You for perfecting everything concerning me. Lead and guide me in every area of my life. I trust Your plans for me and place my life in Your hands. In the mighty name of Jesus, Amen.

Day 22

~ DO NOT BE ANXIOUS ~

Day 22

DO NOT BE ANXIOUS

"Do not be anxious about anything, but in every situation, by prayer and petition, with thanksgiving, present your requests to God."
Philippians 4:6

Why pray and believe God for apples and then settle for oranges? If you are believing God for an apple, wait on the apple. Do not be duped into a counterfeit orange just because it is a fruit. Do not be anxious. Learn patience, and how to wait for the manifestation of promises in your life.

Prayer: Father, in the name of Jesus, remove all anxiety from me. I am trusting in You for every promise concerning my life. I will await the promise, and dismiss any counterfeit. In the mighty name of Jesus, Amen.

Day 23

~WRITE THE VISION ~

Day 23

WRITE THE VISION

"Write down the revelation and make it plain on tablets so that a herald may run with it"
Habakkuk 2:2

Have you taken time to think of a long term plan for your new career? One major career milestone is accomplished by simply finishing and working in your calling as a nurse. Do you have other dreams and goals? If your dreams and goals don't scare you, then you are likely dreaming too small! Sometimes we get caught up in how it will work or how to accomplish the goal. In those instances, we allow negative self-talk and fear to stop us from going for our goals. When God places the dream or vision inside of you, He already has a plan of how to help you make it happen. Start the plan today by simply writing the vision, and making it plain.

Prayer: Father, in the name of Jesus, help me to write the vision and make it plain. Dispatch angels on my behalf to help bring every promise forth for my life. In the mighty name of Jesus, Amen.

Day 24

~ BEING THANKFUL ~

Day 24

BEING THANKFUL

"Devote yourselves to prayer, being watchful and thankful."
Colossians 4:2

Each and every day, with the challenges that life brings, it is easy to become complacent and ungrateful. Can you remember the days you prayed so hard to receive the blessings you now have? Frustration, stress, and exhaustion are all challenges experienced by new nurses. In such times, it is important to be thankful. The days are long, and the work is mentally draining, but you must be thankful. Over time, you will find out that the more thankful you become, the more God will give you to be thankful for.

Prayer: Father, in the name of Jesus, I am so thankful to you. Help me each and every day to glorify your name with a heart of thanksgiving. In the mighty name of Jesus, Amen.

Day 25

~STICK WITH IT ~

Day 25

STICK WITH IT

"Do you not know that in a race all the runners run, but only one gets the prize? Run in such a way as to get the prize"
I Corinthians 9:24

Can you remember the first time you attempted an IV? How about the first time you inserted a Foley catheter? Then the first time, a patient's condition deteriorated in front of you? It is overwhelming, and feelings of doubt, insecurity and fear are common. In such times, it is important to stick with it. As time goes on and you continue in your work, skills become easier, confidence is gained, and doubt is lessened. There is no designated timeline of when things becomes better, but it does become easier each and every shift. Just stick with it!

Prayer: Father, in the name of Jesus work through my hands. Help me to learn new skills, and become better equipped to serve in my calling each and every day. In the mighty name of Jesus, Amen.

Day 26

~ FORGET FEAR ~

Day 26

FORGET FEAR

"For the Spirit God gave us does not make us timid, but gives us power, love and self-discipline."
2 Timothy 1:7

Going home after a long shift and wondering if you charted everything, did you complete all your tasks and if your patient will be there tomorrow is a great source of fear for new nurses everywhere. However, this experience is not unique to the new nurse as veteran nurses often experience the same overwhelming feelings of inadequacy. In time, the fears and doubt occur to a lesser degree, but yet remain a consistent part of our experience in the nursing workforce. During times when fear steps in, remember the word of God, fear does not come from God.

Prayer: Father, in the name of Jesus, thank You for taking away all fear. Help me to remember victory through the blood of Jesus. I will not fear, and I will trust Your perfect will concerning my life. In the mighty name of Jesus, Amen.

Day 27

~ THE LORD IS GOOD ~

Day 27

THE LORD IS GOOD

"Taste and see that the Lord is good; blessed is the one who takes refuge in him."
Psalm 34:8

Taking time to get to know God in a more intimate and more personal way changes your outlook on everything. As you begin to know Him as more than a simple gift giver, or someone to call when in need, then will He open His heart up more to you. God is the creator of all, and His ways are excellent. As you begin to offer praise and thanksgiving to God, He will empower and equip you to face any obstacles or challenges that come your way. Take time and get to know Him in a more intimate way.

Prayer: Father, in the name of Jesus, teach me Your ways. I desire to know You in a more intimate way. Reveal to me the great mysteries of Your word, and the power of the cross trough Jesus. In the mighty name of Jesus, Amen.

Day 28

~ DON'T FORGET SELF-CARE ~

Day 28

DON'T FORGET SELF-CARE

"Dear friend, I pray that you may enjoy good health and that all may go well with you, even as your soul is getting along well"
3 John: 2

You've finished nursing school, and started your calling, great! Many times, after completing a huge milestone such as nursing school, we do not take time to simply rest. Often, the financial challenges experienced while in nursing school make it necessary to enter into the workforce immediately. However, it remains of the utmost importance to take care of yourself. During the time when you are off, take the time to rest. It will be difficult for you to function at an optimum level if you are exhausted and stressed. As God prospers you financially, pray today to prosper in health as well.

Prayer: Father, in the name of Jesus, help me to prosper in all things. Lord, touch my body and increase my health. Help me to take care of myself spiritually, physically, and emotionally. In the mighty name of Jesus, Amen.

Day 29

~ COPING WITH DEATH ~

Day 29

COPING WITH DEATH

"Blessed are those who mourn, for they will be comforted"
Matthew 5:4

Death is an inevitable part of life. As nurses, we work diligently to protect our patients and keep them alive. Sadly, in spite of our best efforts our patients sometimes die. Ask any nurse, and they will have that one patient they will always remember. Death leaves a sting, and hurts us to the core. Coping with the death of your first patient is difficult. In these times, you question your actions as a nurse, and try to recollect if you have done all you could. During such times, it is important to seek the father, allow Him to help you through this difficult process.

Prayer: Father, in the name of Jesus strengthen me during times of loss. Help me to serve as a comforter for those who mourn. Prepare me to share Your compassion in my daily life. In the mighty name of Jesus, Amen.

Day 30

~ A GOOD REPORT ~

Day 30

"Moreover he must have a good report of them which are without; lest he fall into reproach and the snare of the devil"
1 Timothy 3:7

As any nurse will tell you "if it wasn't documented, then it was not done." In your role, remember the essence of this adage in all that you do. As a nurse you are entrusted with confidential information, and patients in their most vulnerable states. Your name, and your position as an individual, will collectively make up your character as a nurse. Remember the need to have a "good reputation". Let your documentation be performed in such a manner that it will protect you in the event that you become ensnared in a legal or court system. Take time today to allow God to help you remember your character, the necessity of providing oncoming nurses with a good report, and the need to cover yourself adequately in your documentation.

Prayer: Father, in the name of Jesus help my work and personal life to glorify You. Lord, I desire to please You in every area of my life. In all that I do, help me to maintain a good report. In the mighty name of Jesus, Amen.

Prayers

Dear Nurse

Dear Nurse:

I would love to tell you that each day will be amazing, all medications will be given on time, and all of your patients ambulatory. However, there will be days when you question if you did everything, and you will hear call lights in your sleep. On those days, please do not lose hope! Here's a little dose of hope for those hopeless days!

Scriptures to Renew Hope

- But those **who hope in the Lord will renew their strength**. They will soar on wings like eagles; they will run and not grow weary, they will walk and not be faint. **(Isaiah 40:31)**
- And the God of all grace, who called you to his eternal glory in Christ, after you have suffered a little while, will **himself restore you and make you strong, firm and steadfast.**(I Peter 5:10)
- And **hope does not put us to shame**, because God's love has been poured out into our hearts through the Holy Spirit, who has been given to us. **(Romans 5:5)**
- May the **God of hope** fill you with all joy and peace as you trust in Him, so that you may **overflow with hope by the power of the Holy Spirit. (Romans 15:13)**
- Oh, that **I might have my request**, God would grant **what I hope for**. (Job 6:8)
- Be strong and take heart, all you **who hope in the Lord. (** Psalm 31:24)
- Trust **in the Lord with all your heart** and lean not on your

own understanding in all your ways submit to Him, and **he will make your paths straight**. **(Proverbs 3:5-6)**

- **Peace I leave with you; my peace I give you**. I do not give to you as the world gives. **Do not let your hearts be troubled and do not be afraid**. **(John 14:27)**
- For the Spirit God gave us does not make us timid, **but gives us power, love and self-discipline. (2 Timothy 1:7)**

Salvation Prayer

Father God, I have tried it my way and failed. I know that I am a sinner in need of salvation. No longer will I do it my way, I ask You to take the lead and guide me throughout my life. In faith, I accept the gift of salvation made possible through the precious blood of Jesus on the cross. I now accept You as Lord and Savior of my life. Thank You father for sending Jesus. I believe that You, Jesus are the son of God who died on the cross for my sins and rose from the dead on the third day. Thank You for bearing my sins, and the cross that I could not bear. Thank You for the gift of eternal life. I believe Your words are true, and I accept You as the power source in my life. Come into my heart, Lord Jesus and be my savior.

Amen

7 Keys to building your Relationship with the Holy Spirit

- **Become aware:** make yourself aware, He lives on the inside of you and He longs to commune with you daily. **"And I will ask the Father, and He will give you another advocate to help you and be with you forever— the Spirit of truth. The world cannot accept Him, because it neither sees Him nor knows Him.** *But you know Him, for He lives with You and will be in You.*(**John 14:16-17)**
- **Believe:** believing is very important. Unbelief hinders the very possibility of your prayers and relationship with him. And without faith it is impossible to please God, because *anyone who comes to Him must believe that He exists and that He rewards those who earnestly seek Him.* **(Hebrews 11:6).**
- **Worship:** worship is the key that unlocks the door into His presence. Take time to worship Him not for what He has or can do for you, but simply because of who He is. Enter His gates with thanksgiving and His courts with praise; *give thanks to Him and praise His name.* **(Psalm 100:4)**
- **Prayer:** prayer is an important component of daily fellowship. Pray and speak His promises and will for your

life. His promises and will are found in the word of God. This is the confidence we have in approaching God: that *if we ask anything according to his will, He hears us.*(**1 John 5:14)**

- **Spend time with Him:** take the initiative to carve out time daily to get to know him. Learn His voice and pursue Him **(He is a person, not an IT or THING!!)** When the Advocate comes, whom I will send to you from the Father —the Spirit of truth who goes out from the Father—*He will testify about me.* **(John 15:26)**
- **Have no other God before him**: He is the only one who can fill all of Your voids. He is the answer to everything you have ever desired or longed for. The fullness of joy is found with Him. Jesus replied: "*Love the Lord your God with all your heart and with all your soul and with all your mind.*(Matthew 22:37)
- **Avoid behaviors that grieve Him:** grieving Him extends beyond the obvious fleshly sins that we ordinarily think on. Grieving Him can occur when we do not love right, when we walk in unforgiveness, when we gossip, and when we choose to live our lives in an unholy manner. We must make the choice daily to embrace His love, seek forgiveness, and be cleansed continuously in the precious blood of Jesus. And *do not grieve the Holy Spirit of God*, with whom you were sealed for the day of redemption. **(Ephesians 4:30)**

Prayer For Confidence

Father God, I recognize Your calling on my life as a nurse. I am so grateful to You for allowing me the opportunity to fulfill my dream, and work in my calling. Lead and guide me each day, and increase my confidence. Help me each and every day to nurse from the heart while using my mind, and allow my hands to be used as an instrument of Your glory. Father, increase my knowledge and assist me in learning each and every day. Teach me that which I do not know. Thank you for being the great teacher, and healer. I will continuously bless Your name, in the mighty name of Jesus I pray,

Amen

Prayer for Nurses

Father God, in the name of Jesus, You are the source of my strength and I thank You for my divine calling to serve others. Equip me to serve each day with the humility of Christ. Help me to comfort all who are in need, and give me wisdom with my words. When I am unsure of my direction, help me to seek Your wisdom, and find comfort in You. Open my heart to the needs of others and help me to provide compassionate care when it is needed most. Let me display Your love and serve as Your hands and feet here on earth, in the mighty name of Jesus,

Amen

Prayer For Encouragement

Heavenly father, thank You for taking the lead in my life. Thank You for being here when I am lost, discouraged and afraid. Help me to be renewed in heart, and mind each and every day. Encourage my heart through Your word. Lord, grant me strength to make it through this day. I will forever sing your praises, in Jesus mighty name,

Amen

Made in the USA
Las Vegas, NV
31 May 2022

49614618R00085